CLIMBING THE HIMALAYAN MOUNTAINS

Sonya Newland

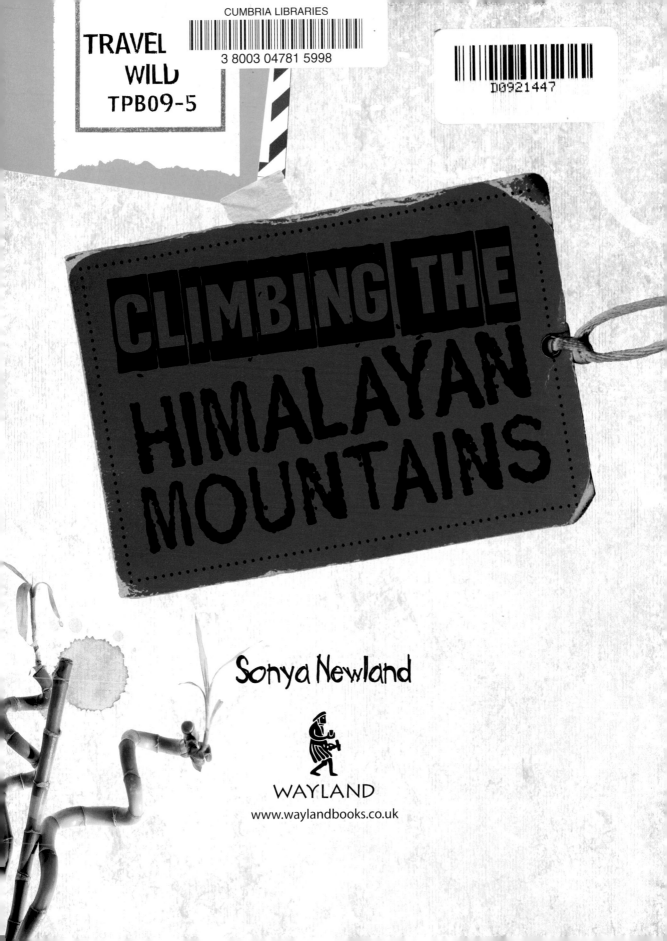

WAYLAND
www.waylandbooks.co.uk

Published in Great Britain in 2018
by Wayland

Copyright © Wayland, 2016

ISBN: 978 0 7502 9863 6
10 9 8 7 6 5 4 3 2 1

Wayland
An imprint of
Hachette Children's Group
Part of Hodder & Stoughton
Carmelite House
50 Victoria Embankment
London EC4Y 0DZ

An Hachette UK Company
www.hachette.co.uk
www.hachettechildrens.co.uk

MIX
Paper from
responsible sources
FSC® C104740

A catalogue for this title is available from
the British Library

Printed and bound in China

Produced for Wayland by
White-Thomson Publishing Ltd
www.wtpub.co.uk

Author: Sonya Newland
Designer: Rocket Design (East Anglia) Ltd
Picture researcher: Izzi Howell
Map: Stefan Chabluk
Wayland editor: Elizabeth Brent

CONTENTS

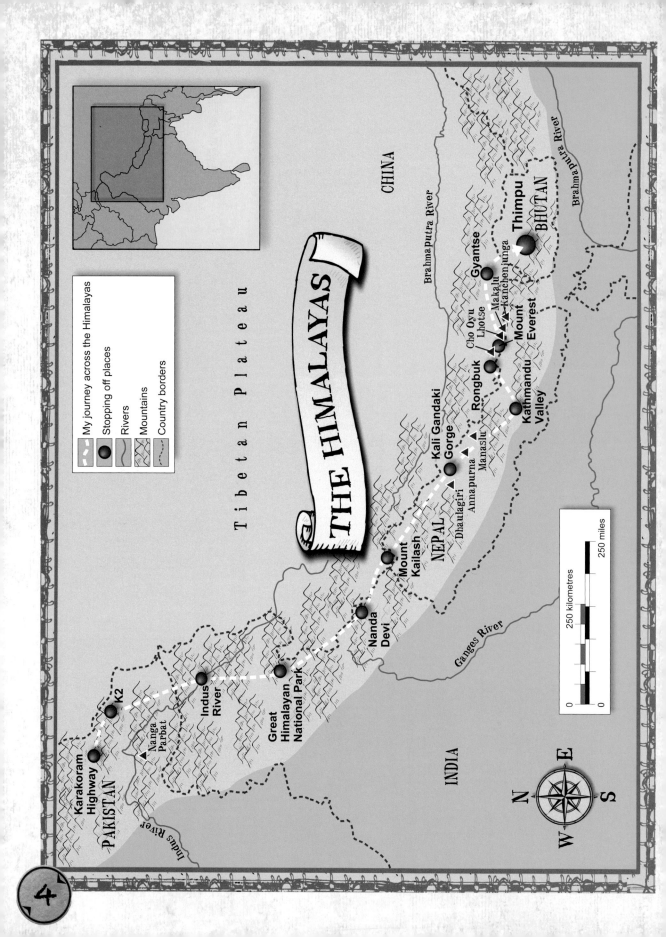

THE HIMALAYAN MOUNTAINS

Preparing for the trip

I'm finally on my way! Tomorrow I'll be setting off for western China, where I'll begin my amazing adventure through the Himalayan mountains. I've been training for months so I'll be ready to walk the long distances, but I know that it's still going to be a tough journey at high altitude. I'm ready for the challenge though — this is going to be the trek of a lifetime!

The Himalayan range

The Himalayan mountains form a 2,500-km curve, stretching east to west through five countries — China (including Tibet), Pakistan, India, Nepal and Bhutan. The mountains are bordered in the north by the massive Tibetan Plateau. Several Indian states, as well as Nepal and Bhutan, lie on the southern slopes. The Himalayas are home to nine of the ten highest mountains in the world, including the very highest peak, Mount Everest.

When to go

Summer in the Himalayas is monsoon season, so I've decided to start my journey in October. It will always be cold higher up in the mountains, but it should be pleasant travelling on the lower routes. Autumn is also better than spring because the weather is usually clear all day at this time of year. In spring, cloud often builds up in the afternoons.

Equipment

I've decided to bring along the following:

- hat
- walking boots
- fleece
- waterproof gloves
- first aid kit
- map and compass
- sun cream
- torch with extra batteries
- whistle
- wraparound sunglasses
- signalling mirror
- matches
- water bottle
- sleeping bag
- binoculars

GROWING MOUNTAINS

11 October
Karakoram Highway
to the Khunjerab Pass

I'm here at last! Arriving in China yesterday, I immediately set off for the Karakoram Highway. This long road links China and Pakistan across the Karakoram mountains – a separate mountain range that lies to the far west of the Himalayas. The bus journey to the Pakistan border was scary – the highway is very narrow in places and I was afraid we might plummet down the steep mountainside! But the views all around were incredible, with jagged mountain peaks as far as the eye could see.

Fold mountains

The Himalayas are fold mountains. This type of mountain forms when giant pieces of the earth's crust, called tectonic plates, collide, which forces their edges upwards. Over millions of years, the sharp rocky edges build up into mountains. The Himalayas are still growing at a rate of about 1 cm every year!

The Himalayas began to form about 50 million years ago.

The Karakoram Highway

Today, the 1,300-km-long Karakoram Highway is the highest paved road in the world. Thousands of years before the highway was built, however, this route through the mountains was part of the ancient Silk Road. It was used by traders making the long journey from the East to the West to sell their goods.

Be smart, survive!

High up in the mountains there is less oxygen in the air than there is lower down. This makes it harder to breathe. If you're going to be trekking high up, spend a few days gaining altitude slowly, so your body gets used to the thinner air gradually. Climb high during the day, but sleep lower down if possible to give your body a chance to recover at night.

Crossing crevasses

Snow bridges are drifts of snow that build up over a crevasse. They might look solid, but they can easily crack  under the weight of a person, and you could fall right through. Wherever you go in the mountains, watch where you are treading. Use a pole to tap the snow ahead of you to make sure it won't crumble beneath your feet.

The Khunjerab Pass

At 4,800 m, the Khunjerab Pass is the highest border crossing in the world — and the highest point on the Karakoram Highway. The pass marks the boundary between China and Pakistan, but it is not always possible to cross between the two countries here. Between November and May, this part of the highway is often blocked by snow.

18 October
Khunjerab Pass
to K2

I've made camp on the Baltoro Glacier, with views up the steep and stormy slopes of the mountain K2. It's freezing here, and I'm shivering so much that I can hardly write! The landscape and the weather are a real change from the past few days, when I've been trekking through the Hunza Valley. It's still warm and green there at this time of year.

K2

At 8,611 m, K2 is the second–highest mountain in the world. It is named K2 because it was the second mountain in the Karakoram range to be measured. Most mountains also have a local name, and K2 is sometimes called Chogori, which means 'Big Mountain'. Although K2 is not as high as Everest, its steep slopes are much more difficult to climb and there are frequent storms. Far fewer people have reached the summit of K2 than of Everest.

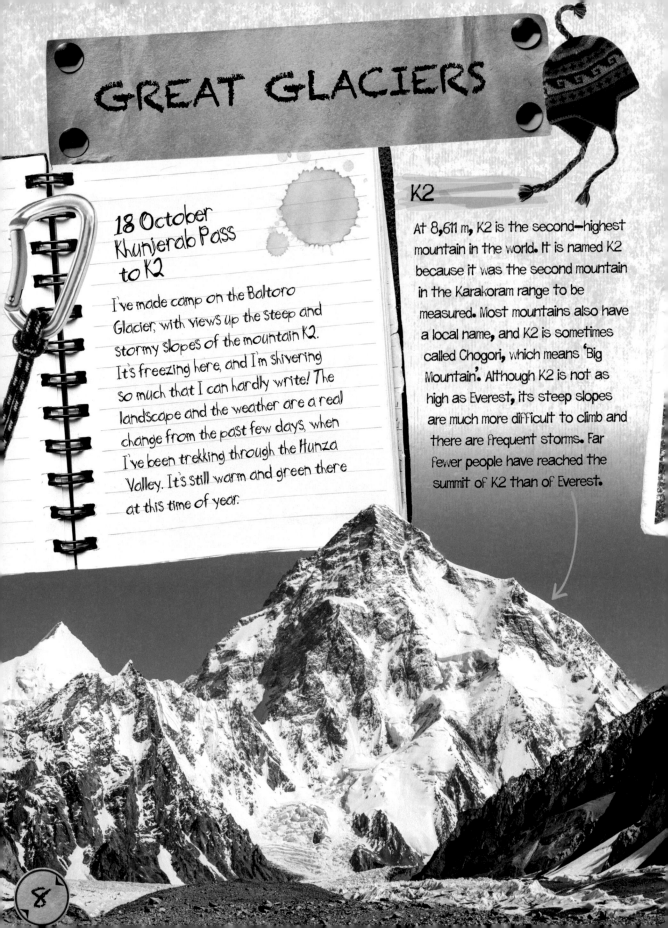

The Baltoro Glacier

A glacier is a large, slow-moving river of ice that forms in high mountain regions. The Baltoro Glacier is one of the largest in the world – so big, in fact, that it can be seen from space! It begins at a place called Concordia, at the foot of K2. From here it flows for more than 60 km through the Karakoram mountains. Another glacier, the Godwin–Austen, meets the Baltoro at Concordia.

Be smart, survive!

Temperatures can drop below freezing in the mountains at night, so I build a camp fire to keep warm (and to cook my dinner). I collect wood and pile it into a cone shape. If I can find leaves or dry grass I put some in the middle of the fire to act as kindling. I use matches, kept in a waterproof container, to light the fire.

Avalanche danger

Avalanches kill more than 150 people every year. If you find yourself caught in an avalanche, follow these steps to escape:

1 Try to move to the side of the avalanche if you see one coming.
2 Drop your equipment – you don't want to be weighed down by a heavy pack.
3 Swim! Moving your arms and legs to swim in the snow will help you stay near the surface.
4 Keep as much space as possible around your face so you have some air to breathe and will avoid suffocation.
5 If you are getting buried in snow, stick one arm up above your head in the direction of the surface. This will help you know which way is up, and may help rescuers find you.

HIMALAYAN RIVERS

24 October
K2 to the Indus River

The mountains and glaciers in the Karakoram were spectacular, but it was hard work walking in that frozen landscape. I'm happy to be making my way south-eastwards towards the border between Pakistan and India. Yesterday I reached the Indus River, so I gave my feet a rest and went rafting! As I glided along the water, my guide told me all about the three great rivers that begin in the Himalayas.

The Indus

The Indus River begins in the Tibetan Plateau and runs for about 3,000 km through Tibet, Pakistan and India. It flows all the way to the Arabian Sea. Through the Himalayas, the Indus has carved out a huge gorge, more than 5,000 m deep, near Nanga Parbat — the ninth—highest mountain in the world.

Hindu sadhus (holy men) bathe in the freezing waters at the source of the River Ganges.

The Ganges

According to legend, the River Ganges was created by the Hindu god Vishnu, and followers of this religion believe the river is sacred. It actually begins in an ice cave on the Gangotri Glacier, which lies in the Indian state of Uttarakhand. Many Hindus make a pilgrimage to this place. The Ganges flows for more than 2,000 km through much of India.

Drinking water

If you run out of water and aren't anywhere near a river or stream, don't eat handfuls of snow! You might think that frozen water is okay, but eating it can cause your body temperature to drop to dangerously low levels. Always find a container and melt the snow or ice before you drink it.

The Brahmaputra

Starting near the Chemayungdung Glacier in south-western Tibet, the Brahmaputra runs eastwards through the Himalayas. It eventually meets the Ganges and the two rivers form a huge delta that flows into the Bay of Bengal.

WILD ANIMALS

28 October
The Indus River to the Great Himalayan National Park

I haven't seen many people on my travels so far, but I'm definitely not alone! On the rocky slopes I've seen plenty of sure-footed animals such as sheep and goats, and I've even caught a glimpse of the beautiful, rare snow leopard. Now that I've crossed into India, I'm spending a few days in the Great Himalayan National Park in the hope of seeing and learning more about the many creatures that make their home here in the mountains.

Snow leopards

These mountain cats grow up to 1.5 m long and can kill animals that are more than three times their own weight! They usually prey on the blue sheep, or bharal, and the mountain ibex that are found high in the Himalayas. However, snow leopards sometimes attack livestock, so many of them have been killed by farmers and herders protecting their animals. Because of this, snow leopards are now an endangered species.

Himalayan mammals

Several large species of mammal live in the foothills of the Himalayas. Asian black bears climb quite high in the mountains in the warmer summer months, but they spend the winter in the tropical forests lower down. Indian rhinos live in the Terai region of India at the base of the Himalayas, but hunting and habitat destruction are starting to threaten them too. Tigers can also be found in low regions of the Himalayas, in both India and further east, in Bhutan.

Yaks

These large, long-haired animals are related to cows. They are extremely hardy and can survive in some of the most difficult mountain landscapes. There are small populations of wild yaks in the Himalayas, but most have been domesticated. The local people raise them as livestock or use them as pack animals.

Asian black bears are also known as moon bears because of the light patch on their chest that looks like a crescent moon.

Yak attack!

The people who live in the Himalayas use yaks to carry loads up and down the mountains. These large beasts will sometimes charge along at speed and won't stop for anything in their way – even people! If you see one coming, always move towards the mountain side rather than the edge of the trail, so you don't get pushed off the mountain by the charging animal.

PLANTS AND FLOWERS

4 November
Great Himalayan National Park to Nanda Devi

I've set up camp in sight of the twin peaks of Nanda Devi, the third-highest mountain in India. The national park that surrounds the mountain is home to snow leopards, black bears, deer and the goat-like Himalayan tahr, among many other creatures. But it is the plants and flowers that have really amazed me on my journey here. Autumn is setting in but many mountain plants are still flourishing, particularly in the lower regions.

People who live in the lower parts of the Himalayas cut down bamboo to use as a building material.

Forest zones

There are four 'zones' of vegetation in the Himalayas: tropical evergreen forests, subtropical deciduous forests, temperate forests and alpine meadows. The evergreen forests lie at around 1,200 m. Here there are bamboo, pine and palm trees. The deciduous forests can be found at around 2,200 m and are made up of trees such as oak and magnolia.

High forests and meadows

The temperate forests rise another 500 m up the mountain slopes. Cedar, maple, spruce and birch trees all grow here. The alpine zone is the highest area where plants grow in the Himalayas. Alpine meadows can be found at up to 5,000 m, but higher than this there is nothing but rocks and snow.

Nanda Devi and the Valley of Flowers

The rugged mountain landscape around Nanda Devi contrasts with the Valley of Flowers that I passed through to get here. This Indian valley was sprinkled with snow when I arrived, but between July and September it is carpeted with stunning wildflowers. Orchids, rhododendrons, poppies and many other species of plant grow in this high Himalayan valley.

Be smart, survive!

The Himalayas are wild and largely unpopulated. If you get lost or into any kind of difficulty, help might be a long way off. To avoid getting into trouble, stay on the roads or marked walking trails along mountain routes. Never venture off on your own - even if you're sure you know the way, others may not be able to find you if you hurt yourself and can't make it back.

SACRED PLACES

7 November
Nanda Devi to Mount Kailash

Many of the mountains in the Himalayan range are considered sacred. Some people of the Himalayas believe that the peaks reach so high that they touch the realm of the gods. They think the mountains are a link between the world of humans below and the heavens above. Mount Kailash is one of the most spiritual places in the Himalayas, and the sight of this great mountain rising high in the clear, cold, silent air is certainly awe-inspiring.

Mount Kailash

This 6,714-m-high mountain is a holy place for followers of Hinduism, Buddhism and Jainism. People have made pilgrimages to this sacred spot since ancient times, believing it is linked to some of the most important figures in their religion. For Hindus, Kailash is home to Lord Shiva, while Buddhists think that the god Chakrasamvara lives there. Jains believe that Kailash was where the great teacher Rishaba was finally freed from the cycle of death and rebirth.

Some Buddhist pilgrims go all the way around the base of Mount Kailash on their stomachs.

Snow blindness

Snow blindness is caused by the glare of bright sunshine reflecting off the snow in high mountain regions. It may just cause your eyes to feel gritty and make your vision a bit blurred, but at worst you can temporarily lose your sight completely. Always wear good-quality wraparound sunglasses, and reduce the glare by smearing soot from the ashes of your camp fire under your eyes.

GET OUT ALIVE !!

Bon

Before Buddhism came to Tibet in the seventh century CE, the people of this region belonged to a religion called Bon. Around 100,000 Tibetans still follow this religion, although it now includes elements of Buddhism. Like Buddhists, Bonpos believe that Mount Kailash is a holy place – the site of a battle between the shaman Naro Bon–chung and the Buddhist wise man Milarepa.

17

HIGHS AND LOWS

22 November
Mount Kailash to Kali Gandaki Gorge

Leaving Mount Kailash behind me, I crossed into Nepal and began the 400-km journey to the Kali Gandaki Gorge. It's been a long trek through some difficult terrain. But it was worth every step to get here, to have the chance to go white-water rafting on the Gandaki River and to venture across a narrow rope bridge strung perilously over the gorge, all in the shadow of the towering Annapurna.

Be smart, survive!

Before setting off on a long and difficult journey like a trek through the Himalayas, it is important to prepare yourself. Making sure you are physically fit is a good start, but you should also prepare mentally. Before you leave, think about the parts of your journey that might scare you - for example, heights, extreme cold or fear of wild animals. Anticipating your fears will build your confidence in dealing with them when the time comes. It also helps to have a positive attitude!

Kali Gandaki Gorge

The Kali Gandaki is the Gandaki River, which flows for 630 km, carving an immense gorge through the Himalayas in this part of Nepal. The Kali Gandaki Gorge is the deepest in the world, plunging to depths of 5,571 m. It is bordered by two of the world's ten-highest mountains – Dhaulagiri (No. 7) in the west and Annapurna I (No. 10) in the east. The river that runs through the gorge is older than the mountains themselves.

The Annapurna

The Annapurna is a group of mountains in the Nepalese Himalayas. The group consists of three main peaks (Annapurna I Main, Central and East) and five smaller ones. There are only 14 mountains on earth that are higher than 8,000 m, and Annapurna I is famous for being the first one that was successfully climbed. French mountaineers Maurice Herzog and Louis Lachenal reached the summit of this 'eight-thousander' in June 1950.

27 November
Kali Gandaki Gorge to
Kathmandu Valley

I'm spending a few days at a tea house in the Kathmandu Valley, not far from Kathmandu, the capital of Nepal. I had a wonderful day yesterday, exploring the ancient buildings in this fascinating city. When I got back I had lots of questions for the friendly Nepalese family that runs the lodge and they told me all about the local culture. It seems that the Himalayan people are as varied as the landscape itself, and each valley has its own style of buildings, traditions and distinctive dress.

The Kathmandu Valley covers 570 square km in the central Himalayas. The people who live in this part of the mountains, the Newar, follow both Hinduism and Buddhism, and there are ancient sacred sites for both religions in the valley. Some of these, including the famous pagoda temples, were established by the kings that ruled this region as long ago as the 4th century CE.

Sherpas

The Sherpas come from the Khumbu Valley, in the mountainous region around Everest in eastern Nepal. Because they live their whole lives so high up, Sherpas are not affected by the altitude. They are also skilled mountaineers, so they often work as guides for visitors. Many Sherpas have died helping others to achieve their dream of reaching the top of Everest and other Himalayan mountains.

Be smart, survive!

When camping in the mountains, make sure you pitch your tent carefully. Don't set up camp in or near dry riverbeds, and avoid places that might be at risk of rock falls or avalanches. Find level ground to sleep on when you can. If you have to sleep on an incline, never have your head pointing downhill. It's important to stay warm at night, so use a mat or another layer of some kind to keep your sleeping bag off the ground. Wear extra clothes if necessary.

The yeti

Some Himalayan tribespeople believe in the yeti — a creature a bit larger than a man and covered in hair. Followers of the Bon religion believed in a wild man whose blood was needed for certain rituals. Most people think that the yeti is just a myth, but some visitors to the Himalayas have seen large footprints in the snow, or have caught a glimpse of something that looks like a large ape ...

21

BUDDHISM IN TIBET

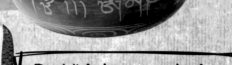

29 November
Kathmandu Valley to Rongbuk

From Kathmandu, I headed north-east towards the Chinese region of Tibet and jumped on the Friendship Highway – an 800-km-long road running from the border between Tibet and Nepal to the Tibetan capital of Lhasa. I'm off to Mount Everest, but on my way to this legendary landmark I've stopped at the famous Rongbuk Monastery. Some of the earliest Everest explorers stayed here on their journey and received blessings from the lama to keep them safe on the mountain.

Buddhist monasteries

All over the Himalayas, monasteries have been built into the mountainsides. Inside them, Buddhist monks live simple lives and carry out religious practices such as meditation. When the first explorers came to Rongbuk in the 1920s, it was a thriving monastery. Sadly it was destroyed in the 1970s and although it is now rebuilt, only a few monks live here. In the cliff walls surrounding the monastery are caves where monks used to live when they wanted to spend time completely alone.

Buddhist traditions

In many places on my journey, I've seen strings of colourful prayer flags strung across the mountains. These have mantras (repeated words or sayings) and prayers written on them. Tibetan Buddhists believe that the prayers are carried out into the world when the wind blows the flags.

Hypothermia and frostbite

Hypothermia is one of the most serious threats to people climbing in the mountains.
It happens when your body temperature drops too low. Symptoms include shivering uncontrollably and not being able to think clearly. Sometimes people can become unconscious or even die. If someone in your party is suffering from hypothermia, put them in a warm sleeping bag and make them drink hot, sweet liquids. It is important that they warm up gradually, though. Heating up too fast can cause heart failure.

GET OUT ALIVE!!

Sky burials

Many Tibetans believe that when someone dies, their spirit takes on a new form. Their old body is no longer required, so there is no need to preserve it in any way, or bury it as people might do in other cultures.
The Tibetans carry out 'sky burials'. They leave dead bodies on the top of mountains to be disposed of in a natural way.

CLIMBING EVEREST

WAY TO M.T. EVEREST B.C.

1 December
Rongbuk to Mount Everest

Back on the Friendship Highway, I made the quick ascent to the famous Everest Base Camp. I'm not going to try and reach the summit, but I couldn't miss the chance to get so close to this mighty mountain! May is the most popular time for people to climb Everest, but even in December, Base Camp is packed with trekkers who, like me, have come to look in awe at the highest point on the planet.

The 'Mother Goddess'

Lying on the border between Nepal and Tibet, Everest reaches almost 8,850 m into the clouds – it is the highest mountain on earth. Its name in Tibetan is Chomolungma, which means 'Mother Goddess of the World'. It is shaped like a three-sided pyramid and each side has a name: the North Face, the East Face and the Southwest Face. Around the base of Everest are several huge glaciers, including the Khumbu.

The Khumbu Glacier at the base of Everest is the highest glacier in the world.

Expeditions to Everest

The first expeditions to Everest by westerners were made in the 1920s. People came to map the area and to work out the best route to the top. Early attempts to climb the mountain ended in failure, though, and many men died. It was only in 1953 that Edmund Hillary and the Sherpa Tenzing Norgay became the first men to stand on its summit. Since then, hundreds of others have done so — and many more people have also died trying. The part of a mountain above 8,000 m is known as the Death Zone, where there is not enough oxygen for humans to survive for very long.

Edmund Hillary and Tenzing Norgay – the first men to conquer Everest.

Everest climbers set out from Base Camp and climb to the Icefall, at 6,100 m. They make stops at Camp 1, in an area that the first western explorers called the Valley of Silence, then Camps 2 and 3, up to 8,000 m. At Camp 4, the Death Zone begins. From here, climbers trek up the North Ridge and make their way over a series of 'steps' towards the summit. The Hillary Step — a sheer rock face — is the last major obstacle before reaching the top of the world.

Be smart, survive!

There are many perils when mountain climbing. If you are stranded without a tent on a mountainside, build a snow cave for shelter until help arrives. You need to find a snow drift 3-4 m deep, then tunnel into it. About 2.5 m in, start digging up and out to create the cave. Make the ceiling arched so that snow trickles down the sides rather than dripping onto you! Carve a sleeping platform above the entrance, with a trench between the platform and wall so you don't get wet while sleeping.

THE ROOF OF THE WORLD

6 December
Mount Everest to Gyantse

I'm nearly at the end of my incredible journey, but before I head to the last country on my trek I want to see a bit more of Tibet. I've come to Gyantse, a town that lies on an ancient trade route between Tibet and India. The weather has been great for exploring the town and the monasteries that lie further afield. It might be cold here on the Tibetan Plateau, but it's sunny and dry!

The Gyantse Kumbum is the largest stupa (a holy structure) in Tibet.

The Tibetan Plateau

The vast area of the Tibetan Plateau covers about 2.5 million square km. It is known as the 'Roof of the World' because it is so high – nearly 5 km above sea level. It is surrounded on all sides by mountains, including the Himalayas in the south and the Karakoram – where I started my journey – in the west. The whole plateau is dotted with lakes and glaciers.

Monsoon season

Monsoons are Asian winds that change direction according to the season.
In the summer, the monsoons blow from the south—west, bringing heavy rain to southern parts of the Himalayas. The weather may be wet, but it is still warm at this time of year, with temperatures averaging 25 ℃.

Altitude sickness

GET OUT ALIVE!!

This is when the human body cannot cope with the lack of oxygen high up in the mountains. Symptoms include headaches, dizziness, and feeling sick and exhausted. You might feel like you can't breathe properly and have trouble walking. At the first signs of altitude sickness, stop climbing! If the symptoms go away within 24 hours, you can start to climb again. If they don't, get to a lower altitude as soon as possible. Bottled oxygen can improve the symptoms for a short while, too. Take paracetamol to treat the headaches caused by altitude sickness.

The rain shadow effect

The Tibetan Plateau is a rain shadow area. This means that it lies on the sheltered side of the mountains, where no rain falls. Rain is created on the other side of the mountains, but it all falls before the clouds reach the top, so dry air passes down the other side. Rain shadow areas usually have very few plants and flowers because of the lack of rain.

MOUNTAIN KINGDOM

12 December
Gyantse to Thimpu

It's nearly time to leave these amazing mountains behind me. My last stop is Thimpu, in the Kingdom of Bhutan, which is said to be one of the happiest places on earth! I can see why. It's beautiful here - more than half the country is protected as a national park. It's also very peaceful. The Buddhist people of Bhutan seem calm and content. It's the perfect place to relax and reflect on the unbelievable journey I've taken.

Bhutan

The Kingdom of Bhutan is an ancient country on the eastern edge of the Himalayas. Only around 750,000 people live here. Most of them work as farmers, raising crops and livestock such as cattle and yaks. The Bhutanese people all follow a particular type of Buddhism called Vajrayana Buddhism, and there are many Buddhist monasteries. The monks can be identified by their red robes.

The Tiger's Nest

Before I head home, I want to visit one last sacred place in these amazingly spiritual mountains: the Buddhist gompa (fort) known as the Tiger's Nest. Clinging to the side of a cliff, 900 m above the Paro Valley, this is the holiest place in Bhutan. The Bhutanese believe that this is where Buddhism first arrived in the country, brought by the holy man Guru Rinpoche, who flew here on the back of a tiger.

Conserving the Himalayas

The Himalayas are a largely unspoilt part of the world. However, there are environmental problems here. Several species of animals that live in the foothills are dying out because of hunting and because their homes are being destroyed. There are problems around Everest, too, including litter and overcrowding. I hope that people who come here in the future will respect the beauty of the Himalayas and try to keep them that way!

Signal for help

If you get lost or into trouble in the mountains, use a signalling mirror to attract attention. If you hold up a small mirror and move it around, it will catch the sun and make flashes of light that can be seen up to 60 km away. Hopefully someone will spot your signal for help and come to the rescue!

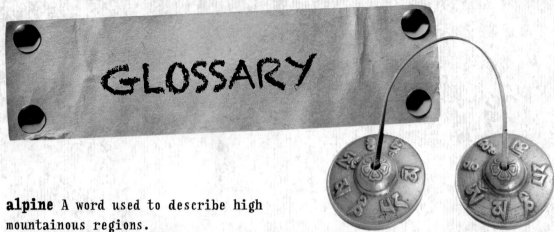

GLOSSARY

alpine A word used to describe high mountainous regions.

altitude How high something is above sea level.

avalanche A large amount of snow, ice and rocks that falls quickly down a mountainside.

deciduous Describes a plant or tree that loses its leaves and grows new ones, depending on the season.

delta A large, flat plain between branches of a river, from where they separate to where they flow into the sea.

domesticated Describes wild animals that have been tamed so they can be raised as livestock.

endangered When there are only a few of a particular type of animal left in the world, so they are in danger of dying out completely.

evergreen Describes a plant or tree whose leaves stay green all year round.

foothills Low hills at the base of a mountain range.

glacier A huge river of ice that moves very slowly.

gorge A narrow valley between mountains, usually with steep, rocky sides and a river running through it.

kindling Small sticks or twigs that burn easily and can be used to start a fire.

lama The religious leader in a Buddhist monastery.

livestock Farm animals that are raised for food or trade.

lodge A house or cabin in the countryside, often made of wood.

meditation The practice of thinking deeply about something.

monsoon Strong winds in southern Asia that blow from the south-west (bringing rain) in the summer and from the north-east in the winter.

myth A traditional story.

pagoda A Hindu or Buddhist temple that usually has several levels, each with an upturned roof.

pilgrimage A journey that people make to a place that is important in their religion.

plateau A large area of high, flat ground.

preserve To take care of something and make sure that it does not rot away.

ritual A religious ceremony involving a particular series of words or actions.

sacred Something that is important in a particular religion.

shaman A holy person who is thought to be able to communicate with the spirit world.

sheer Very steep.

stupa A structure that is considered a holy place by Buddhists and which is used as a place of meditation.

summit The highest point of a mountain.

tectonic plate A giant piece of the earth's crust that moves around very slowly.

terrain A stretch of land and its physical features.

INDEX & FURTHER INFORMATION

Books

Himalayan Mountains (Expedition Diaries) by Simon Chapman (Franklin Watts, 2017)
Mount Everest (Great Planet Earth) by Valerie Bodden (Franklin Watts, 2014)

Websites

http://www.bbc.co.uk/newsround/22702860
http://www.pbs.org/wnet/nature/the-himalayas-himalayas-facts/6341/
http://www.sciencekids.co.nz/sciencefacts/earth/mounteverest.html